Original title:
The Big Bang of Life's Questions

Copyright © 2025 Creative Arts Management OÜ
All rights reserved.

Author: Julian Prescott
ISBN HARDBACK: 978-1-80566-122-1
ISBN PAPERBACK: 978-1-80566-417-8

Mysterious Matter

In a cosmos where socks disappear,
Particles dance, but oh, where's my beer?
Gravity's pulling, but I'm just floating,
Querying life, it feels like I'm noting.

What's hidden in the space between my ears?
Could it be wisdom, or just a few beers?
Mysteries rise like cream in my tea,
Will I find answers or just a funny meme?

Chaotic Harmony

Planets swirl in a jazz band so wild,
Playing odd notes, just like a child.
Why does the sun insist on being bright?
Can I trade a star for just one good night?

Life's a puzzle, missing a piece,
Crammed full of quirks, searching for peace.
Do worms ever wonder, as they squirm by chance,
If they too can join in this cosmic dance?

Shadows of the Unknown

In the dark alleys of thought, we roam,
Is the fridge running, or is it just foam?
Shadows flicker, whispering questions so deep,
Are they wise answers, or just lack of sleep?

Why do we fear what we cannot explain?
Like why my cat thinks I'm its personal plane!
Are ghosts just time-traveling pranks gone wrong?
Or a figment of dreams that don't last long?

Black Holes of Inquiry

The universe yawns, where did it all go?
Swallowed up truths by the cosmic black show.
Is that where my socks end up every night?
What eats the questions, and hides them from sight?

In the voids of our minds, do answers collide?
With quantum hiccups, and curiosity's tide.
Can we launch a probe with just a wise chuckle?
Or will it return with naught but a struggle?

The Birth of Wondering Stars

In the dark, a light did pop,
Questions twinkled, they just won't stop.
Why does cereal float in milk?
Is gravity just a cosmic silk?

Mixing thoughts like cosmic dust,
What's a rocket made of? Rust?
Do aliens drink their tea?
Or are they just too smart for me?

Constellations of Reflection

Wishing on a shooting star,
Why do dreams feel so bizarre?
Can a wish be made with fries?
Or must it come as a surprise?

Maybe stars have wiggly knees,
Not just shining, but full of glee.
If the moon could dance and sing,
Would it wear a diamond ring?

Galaxies of Unanswered Dreams

Whirling thoughts like cosmic stew,
Why can't I find my left shoe?
Do planets gossip in their orbits?
Are comets just celestial squids?

Floating in a sea of haze,
Is space just one big maze?
Where do thoughts go when they hide?
Could they take a cosmic ride?

Cosmic Collisions of Thought

When galaxies bump and collide,
Is it like a rollercoaster ride?
Do they laugh or scream in fright?
Or just toss stars into the night?

Questions whirl like a crazy game,
Is a black hole just too much fame?
Do asteroids have names we know?
Or are they just here to steal the show?

Questing Comets

Comets zoom with a tail of flair,
Seeking answers up in the air.
"Why do we shine?" they jest with glee,
"Is the sun just a star's cup of tea?"

Through the void, they dance and glide,
Chasing mysteries, what a ride!
"Do black holes have snacks to share?"
"Or did they forget their cosmic care?"

Wisdom in the Starlit Silence

Under twinkling skies, we sit and wink,
Galaxies whisper, no time to think.
"What if stars are just sparkly dust?"
"And planets are pizza?" Oh, that's a must!

In the cosmic bakery, we loaf around,
As wisdom in silence, that's where it's found.
"Do aliens giggle when we're not near?"
"Or is their laughter a cosmic sphere?"

The Universe Speaks in Questions

In the grand expanse, questions unfold,
Whispers of wonders, both new and old.
"Is infinity just a really long line?"
"Or is it a riddle wrapped in divine?"

Planets spin with mischievous delight,
"Why do meteorites only sneak at night?"
"Are we all part of a giant game?"
"With hide-and-seek in a cosmic frame?"

Sentient Stars

Stars above flicker with a grin,
"Are we just scribbles in space's kin?"
"Why do we twinkle, what's in a name?"
"Are we just players in a cosmic game?"

They chuckle and hum in their stellar dance,
"If we fall, do we get a second chance?"
"Do we shine brighter when we're feeling fine?"
"Or dim down to nap, in the cosmic line?"

Galactic Gaze

In a vacuum of space, I ponder wide,
Why do socks vanish? Where do they hide?
Stars shine bright in celestial parade,
But my missing left shoe is where I'm dismayed.

Comets zoom by with tails like a kite,
While I'm stuck here, fumbling left and right.
Cosmic wonders, they elude my grasp,
Yet trivia on cats, I awkwardly clasp.

Asteroids crash into the thoughts in my dome,
What's the sound of one hand? A philosophical poem?
Aliens laughing, they watch from afar,
Holding their sides over me, a comedy star!

Galaxies spinning, so vast and so grand,
We barely unpack the chairs for this band.
Life's riddles float like balloons in the sky,
But honestly, why's it so hard to fry?

Twofold Mysteries

Questions arise like toast in the morn,
Did I put the keys down or have they been sworn?
With every tick, my mind goes on roam,
Is this universe vast, or am I alone?

Inquiring minds want to know the score,
Why do I trip on that same kitchen floor?
Like Schrödinger's cat, am I in a fix?
Or simply just snacking on antique mix?

Theories abound, galore in my head,
Why do we fear things that might be dead?
Ghostly pursuits or rumors of cheese,
Confound me more than a sneeze in the breeze!

Life's questions bubble like soda pop fizz,
Is a firefly a bug, or a light-up whiz?
So here we sit, pondering perplexed,
As I break the fourth wall, totally vexed!

The Spectrum of Seeking

Why do we ask, what's the deal?
Like cats with strings, it's all surreal.
Chasing ideas like a game of tag,
With thoughts that burst, sometimes they lag.

Where do socks go in the wash?
Is there a black hole for the posh?
Are aliens laughing at our chase?
Or just sipping tea in outer space?

Inquiring minds, oh what a show,
Seeking truths we still don't know.
With questions that dance like fireflies,
In the vastness where humor lies.

So let's giggle while we ponder,
Through life's riddles, it's quite a wander.
For every question, we'll find a cheer,
And laugh at the cosmic buffet, oh dear!

Life's Cosmic Puzzle

Life's like a puzzle in the stars,
With pieces missing from Jupiter and Mars.
We fit them together like a jigsaw game,
Squeezing in questions, oh what a shame!

Why do ducks quack, is it a spree?
Or are they just trying to make light of me?
The universe giggles, a cosmic prank,
While we find answers, like fish in a tank.

Each piece we grasp is a quirky delight,
Finding humor in shadows and light.
Like socks from laundry that dance in the breeze,
Just when you think you've got it, "Oh, please!"

So let's match our thoughts, side by side,
In this puzzle of life, let's take a ride.
With laughter our guide on this wild quest,
We'll solve it all, or we'll jest!

Starry-eyed Mysteries

Have you heard the stars whisper your name?
Or is that just a trick of the cosmic game?
With twinkling lights, they tease and tease,
Unraveling truths with mischievous ease.

Why is pizza round, cut into wedges?
Do galaxies ponder such hedges?
As we stare into the vast and bright,
Do comets chuckle in sheer delight?

Questions fly like space dust on a spree,
What is love? Is it cosmic debris?
In the grand puzzle, there's humor to find,
Like socks sarcastically leaving you behind.

So let's throw our questions into the void,
With laughter and joy, let's not be annoyed.
As stardust dances, we'll skip and spin,
Embracing the mystery, let the fun begin!

Paradoxes in the Ether

Why is it hard to find a good pen?
Do they vanish like time, now and then?
Paradoxes twirl in a cosmic fed,
With answers like rabbits—poof, they're dead!

Is a truth really true if it bends?
Or do we just laugh at the twists it sends?
Like a diet that's all about cake,
Or a nap that's a mistake for goodness' sake!

With lightyears of questions, we're at a standstill,
Scratching our heads, searching for thrill.
Like the chicken who crossed without a clue,
Just to ponder, "Now what do I do?"

So here's to the mysteries we adore,
With giggles that echo, let's explore!
For in every paradox, humor is found,
In the spacetime of giggles, we're joyously bound!

Questions from the Cosmos

Is there life on Mars, I wonder?
Or is it just a big blunder?
Do black holes hold secrets untold?
Or just socks misplaced in the cold?

Why do stars twinkle at night?
Are they just playing hide and seek right?
Do aliens laugh at our grand schemes?
Or are they asleep, lost in their dreams?

When will gravity take a break?
And let me float like a leaf on the lake?
Can cosmic dust be an artist's muse?
Or is it just the universe's ruse?

What's beyond the edge of it all?
Is it snack time at the cosmic mall?
Will we find answers in silly signs?
Or just a joke written between the lines?

The Origin of Wonder

In the vacuum where questions bloom,
Do thoughts collide with a cosmic boom?
If atoms giggle in the dark,
What kind of dance do they embark?

Do planets sigh in their orbits round?
Or do they just play the dizzy sound?
Is space just a giant game of chess?
With stars as pawns in a cosmic mess?

Why do comet tails stretch and sway?
Are they just showing off their ballet?
If time is a river, what's its flow?
Does it ever stop for a cup of joe?

Are there clouds made of cotton candy?
Or is that thought a bit too dandy?
Why does the sun like to set so bold?
Could it be tired of shining gold?

Stellar Paradoxes

If a tree falls in space, is there sound?
Or is it just silence all around?
What if black holes are just doors to play?
A cosmic club we can't enter today?

Are time machines made of Swiss cheese?
Or do they just trip on cosmic breeze?
If we talk to the cosmos, does it reply?
Or just send back a confused sigh?

Is the universe just a big old joke?
Wrapped in riddles, like puffed-up smoke?
Do supernovas make the best confetti?
Or is that thought a tad too petty?

Why do meteors wish upon stars?
Hoping to reach the land of bizarre?
What if cosmos has a sense of fun?
And laughs with every little sun?

Time's Infinite Canvas

If seconds are painted on a canvas wide,
Do minutes giggle and play inside?
When clocks tick-tock in quirky rhymes,
Are they just bored, counting silly times?

What if memories float as balloons?
Chasing the echoes of forgotten tunes?
Do past and future ever meet?
Or is it just a dance on repeat?

Can time wear silly hats and gowns?
Or is it serious, frowning with frowns?
If I lived in a time-bending dream,
Would I eat cake and jump on a beam?

What if tomorrow comes wrapped in cheer?
And whispers stories we long to hear?
Is every tick a chance to laugh?
Or is it all just a cosmic gaffe?

Celestial Riddles of the Heart

Why did the star refuse to shine?
It thought it was a bit too divine.
Clouds whispered secrets from afar,
While comets giggled as they spar.

Jupiter winked at Mr. Moon,
"Dance with me, let's start this tune!"
But Pluto sighed, quite out of sight,
"I'm just too small for this delight."

Venus blew kisses on the sly,
While Saturn twirled its rings up high.
Mars said, "Hey, pass me the thought!"
But Venus replied, "Not so hot!"

Mercury zoomed with speed so grand,
While Earth just sighed, "This is unplanned."
Life's a riddle in this vast space,
But who would truly want to chase?

Infinite Horizons of Inquiry

Why do clouds never seem to land?
They're busy making air-puff bands.
Questions bounce like raindrops bright,
Chasing shadows, chasing light.

When will the sun finally take a nap?
So stars can play and join the trap.
The moon rolled over with a grin,
"Let's ask the cat — where have you been?"

Lightning giggled with its thunderous boom,
"I'm just here to brighten up the gloom!"
While gentle breezes whispered low,
"Can flowers dream? We'd love to know!"

Time ticks slowly, or flies like a kite,
As owls hoot secrets of the night.
In this circus where thoughts collide,
We joke that wisdom comes outside!

Nebulae of Thought

In a swirl of colorful dust and beam,
Ideas bloom like a wildflower dream.
"What's the speed of a silly thought?"
"Faster than a fish that's caught!"

Planets twirled in a comedic dance,
Each one hoping for a fun romance.
Stars laughed at their long-lost ties,
"Hey, did you hear? We're all the wise!"

Asteroids strolled, quite the sight,
With tales of earthlings in broad daylight.
"What's the biggest question in space?
Is it pizza or just a race?"

As comets dashed past, in a line,
They whispered down, "It's all about time."
In this expanse of giggles so stout,
We ponder what life's all about!

Questions that Dance Among the Stars

Why do stars twinkle, oh so bright?
They're just winking at us with delight.
Satellites gossip while they rotate,
"What's for dinner? It's getting late!"

Through the cosmos, laughter swells,
As planets share their cheeky tales.
"Can a black hole learn to smile?"
"Only if it stretches for a while!"

Galaxies wiggled with a flair,
We read their minds — oh, such a dare!
"Why do meteors always race?"
"To find the best celestial place!"

Questions flutter like butterflies bold,
In a universe that's yet to unfold.
In the vastness where thoughts take flight,
We laugh to ponder day and night!

Stargazer's Dilemma

When I stare at the night sky, oh so wide,
I wonder why socks always seem to hide.
Are there planets where laundry just does itself?
Or do stars collect dust, like books on my shelf?

Is that a comet or just my cat's tail?
Does space travel slow down with old age and frail?
Do aliens giggle at our coffee spills?
Or send us a meme about life's silly thrills?

Essence of the Unknown

What's the secret of life, just a big cosmic joke?
Is it all in the atoms or just in the poke?
Do rabbits hole dive when they ponder their fate?
Or are they just hopping and munching on bait?

Is gravity just a moody friend in disdain?
Tugging at us while we dance in the rain?
Or do black holes simply swallow our snacks?
Leaving us searching for crumbs in the cracks?

Galaxies of Thought

In the cosmos, thoughts spin like whirling stars,
Should I question the universe or just eat candy bars?
Do meteors wish they could slow down and chat?
Or are they in a hurry, yelling, 'What of that?'

Do galaxies giggle at our endless search?
For truth in the chaos of the cosmic church?
Or do they just blink as we float through the void?
Sipping stardust smoothies, utterly overjoyed?

Beyond the Event Horizon

Peeking through the curtain of reality's flair,
I spot a squirrel pondering over its hair.
Is it the universe or just my friend Sue?
Who thinks the world spins based on her to-do?

Do time travelers laugh as they meddle in fate?
Making sure our lunch dates come an hour late?
Or am I just chasing those thoughts on a whim?
Finding out life's best questions are sung out of tune?

Wavelengths of Wonder

In a cosmos of giggles, we float and we glide,
Questions like comets, they zoom and they hide.
Is there life on Mars, or just rocks on the scan?
What's the deal with socks? Where did they all ran?

Dancing through stardust, we twirl in delight,
Why can't we see ghosts if they're out every night?
Tickling the atoms, we laugh with a cheer,
What's the speed of a sneeze? It's faster, I fear!

Blowing bubbles of puzzlement, big and round,
Does a star ever wish it could twirl on the ground?
Why does rain fall up, when it seems to drop down?
A riddle from space in a sparkly gown?

With scale of the universe, it's hard to perceive,
How do you count sheep when they start to weave?
What hides in the depths of a black hole, I prance,
Do particles tango, or merely just dance?

The Void of Understanding

In the depths of void, we ponder and prance,
Is it darkness we fear, or a lack of a chance?
Why does toast always land butter-side down?
And where's the last peanut? It's wearing a crown!

Drifting through nothing, we float like a kite,
Why do we yawn when it's just dawn's light?
How come jam always sticks to the knife?
And what makes a pickle, a pickle in life?

Galaxies giggle, as we chase a round thought,
Does a cat ever ponder the things that we're taught?
Why's the moon so shy, hiding behind the cloud?
A mystery cosmic that draws a big crowd!

In the void of the universe, we chase our own tail,
Is there cheese on the moon? Send a query by mail!
Round and round we spin, with questions so grand,
Echoes of laughter in an endless wonderland!

Gravity of Uncertainty

Falling through space with a comical grace,
What causes gravity? Is it a fun race?
Do fish ever ponder the light that they see?
And which came first—chicken, or just me?

In a black hole's grasp, we bob and we weave,
Can a star get a cold? Does it sneeze and leave?
Why do shoes always pinch at the worst of times?
And why does a rhyme sound a bit like bad crimes?

With questions like balloons floating high in the air,
Where do the socks go when none of us care?
Is the universe grumpy, or is it just shy?
And if stars could talk, would they laugh or would cry?

Caught in the pull of whimsical quests,
Is gravity just nature wearing heavy vests?
The fun of uncertainties keeps growing each day,
As we tumble through wonders, in a silly ballet!

Light of Inquiry

Shining bright beams of questions in flight,
Do photons get lost in the dark of the night?
If light travels fast, what's the hurry, my friend?
And where do the sparks of curiosity end?

In the spectrum of laughter, we giggle and gleam,
Is a rainbow just sunlight that's chasing a dream?
Why does a light bulb always flicker and fade?
And what makes a shadow, just sunlight delayed?

From science-y whims, to a quirk and a grin,
Can time ever tick if no one's clocking in?
Why does a candle turn whispers to glow?
And how does the sun play with warmth down below?

Under the bright whimsy of inquiry's light,
Do questions take naps, or keep buzzing all night?
With winks from the cosmos, we dive into fun,
Counting the wonders as we joyfully run!

Quantum Curiosities

In a universe so grand and wide,
Particles dance with nowhere to hide.
Why do socks vanish in the wash?
Is it a portal or just a nosh?

Quarks play peek-a-boo with my mind,
In a world that's whimsical, yet so blind.
Are cats coiled or merely a ploy?
Let's ponder this with laughter and joy!

Whirlwind of Wistful Thoughts

What if aliens crave pizza from space?
With toppings of stardust, they'd make a great case.
Do trees gossip as the breezes are mild?
Or is silence their game, forever reviled?

Will we ever find the sock in the gloom?
Or is it plotting in a cosmic mushroom?
Questions kidnap our minds, oh so spry,
With each twinkle of stars, a silent sigh.

Echoing Through Eternity

Time echoes back, but it's a little unclear,
I asked my reflection, it just smirked with cheer.
Can a fish ever comprehend the sky?
Or is it merely dreaming as clouds drift by?

Lemons debate with the sweet, sweet honey,
Life's contradictions are rather funny.
If gravity's a force, is it pulling the pranks?
Let's tip our hats to the cosmic janks!

The Light That Asks

A beam of light shines a cheeky grin,
Whispers of wonders caught under its skin.
Why do we text while seated on the throne?
Is there wisdom in pixels, or just monotone?

If planets could laugh, what jests would they tell?
Of black holes and quirks, they'd weave quite a spell.
In the cafe of cosmos, sip on the tease,
For there's humor in questions, if you are at ease.

Celestial Puzzles Unraveled

Why is the sky so vast and blue?
Is that where the missing socks flew?
Can stars be wished upon at night,
Or just celestial balls of light?

If planets dance, do they need pairs?
Do they gossip about us in stares?
When rockets zoom past in a flash,
Are they just playing a cosmic bash?

Does the moon ever feel quite alone?
How does it know when it's time to shone?
If comets have tails, do they shake?
Or do they just swirl in a cosmic quake?

With questions floating like balloons,
And answers hidden in the tunes,
We giggle under cosmic grace,
As we search for wisdom in outer space.

Quantum Quandaries of the Soul

If particles can be both here and there,
Do my thoughts float like they simply don't care?
Is my breakfast really quantum soup,
A swirling enigma inside a groups?

Can a cat choose to be both lost and found?
Or is it part of a mystery profound?
When I try to grasp the meaning of life,
Is there chaos or just quantum strife?

If nothing's ever quite what it seems,
Are we just puppets in someone's dreams?
Oh, the irony of tiny bits,
Sparking questions that give us fits!

In puzzled states, we giggle and sway,
Exploring reality in a playful way,
As probabilistic giggles ignite,
Dancing through the curious night.

Fragments of a Cosmic Mind

Do the stars have a plan for each night?
Or do they just twinkle on a whim of delight?
If the universe expands, what's next on the list?
A cosmic sale? Don't let it be missed!

Why do black holes hide from our view?
Are they the introverts in the cosmic crew?
Do they munch on light like candy so sweet,
Or maybe just crave a good fiery treat?

When galaxies clash with a spark and a boom,
Do they look for a dancefloor or just for a room?
Is there a chart for celestial charades,
Or are cosmic beings just throwing parades?

Let's ponder the wonders, embrace every jest,
As we sift through the cosmos, without any rest,
In fragments of thoughts, we'll giggle and chat,
With humor soaring where silence once sat.

When Stardust Asks

What happens when stardust starts to speak?
Do they have secrets, unique and chic?
Can they ask why we keep changing our styles,
Or ponder over cosmic denial?

Do supernovas throw the best parties,
With fireworks flashing in vast allegories?
Are they sipping starlight like it's a drink,
As they swirl in a galactic wink?

What if aliens laugh at our wild schemes,
And trace our questions like comical beams?
With telescopes tuned to our daily happenings,
Are they just craving a good laugh, or mappings?

So when stardust whispers from up high,
Let's chuckle along and ask, "Oh, why?"
In the laughter of the universe, our questions gleam,
As we float through space on a whimsical dream.

Beyond Space and Time

In the cosmos, questions spin,
Like dust bunnies in a cosmic bin.
Why do socks vanish in the wash?
Are they off to a galactic posh?

What's the secret behind a cat's stare?
Is it wisdom or just a snare?
Why do we chase the ice cream truck?
Maybe it's just a stroke of luck!

Do stars laugh when they ignite?
Or do they dim to hide their fright?
Why do we park on driveways, I ask?
Life's a puzzle, a funny task!

In the galaxy of goosebumps and grins,
We ponder the answers to our whims.
With cosmic giggles, we'll seek and roam,
In this wacky universe we call home!

Fractals of Thought

Questions spiral in fractal delight,
Like mirrors reflecting through day and night.
If time is a circle, can I rewind?
To redo that dance that made me blind?

What if our thoughts had their own GPS?
Guiding us through this mental mess?
If jellybeans can't bounce off a wall,
Will they ever answer the cosmic call?

Do trees gossip when we're not around?
Plotting world domination without a sound?
If laughter's the key, does it need a lock?
Or just hang out with the ticking clock?

In this maze of thoughts, we dawdle and dance,
While sipping tea from a mystic chance.
With each question, our minds take flight,
Chasing answers in the soft moonlight!

The Void's Invitation

In a void where silence makes a sound,
We question why the lost socks are found.
Why do we trip over things unseen?
Is it the universe playing mean?

Does the darkness giggle when we stare?
Or is it plotting who to ensnare?
If an echo trips over its own feet,
Does it laugh, or just face defeat?

What's the deal with gravity's embrace?
It pulls us in, yet keeps us in place.
Why do we fear what we don't understand?
Is it just the invisible hand?

In this void, let laughter resound,
As we seek answers that merrily abound.
With each chuckle, we unravel the gray,
Living absurdly is the best way!

Quantum Questions

In the realm of tiny bits and waves,
Questions jump around like playful knaves.
What came first, the egg or the quark?
Can cats exist in both light and dark?

If time stands still, can I take a nap?
Or does the universe need a map?
How can a thought become a plan?
Is it just magic from a cosmic fan?

Do particles have feelings too?
Or just collide to brew a stew?
If reality's just a fuzzy mess,
Who's the master of this dress?

With each inquiry, we twirl about,
Creating laughter amidst our doubt.
In this quirky dance of what could be,
Let's ponder endlessly and laugh, you see?

Luminescence of Doubt

In the cosmos of thought, we ponder a lot,
Are space cats for real or just a mean plot?
With questions that twinkle like stars in the night,
We chase after answers, but they're just out of sight.

Do aliens wear hats? Do they drink cosmic tea?
Or munch on our snacks while they giggle with glee?
Each notion a spark, some bright, others dim,
In this galaxy of maybes, we leap on a whim.

The Dance of Celestial Questions

Out in the vast void, stars do cha-cha, you see,
While planets all tango, oh what a spree!
Do black holes have parties? Are comets the band?
In this cosmic interpretation, it's totally grand.

Falling through wormholes, we giggle and spin,
With quizzes like meteors that zoom and then grin.
What if space is a playground, where kids all play tag?
In the universe of queries, we never can lag.

Expanding Realms of Consciousness

Mind's a balloon that keeps puffing, it's true,
With thoughts rising up like a wild rendezvous.
Is Schrödinger's cat just a pet with a flair?
Or merely a mime playing hide-and-seek there?

As ideas stretch out, they twist and they twirl,
In this quantum funhouse, our thoughts do a whirl.
Will socks invade space? Will spoons learn to fly?
In this realm of the baffled, we laugh till we cry.

Cosmic Seeds of Knowledge

With seeds of thought planted in minds like a joke,
We garden our doubts, oh the wisdom they stoke!
Do raindrops giggle when they plop on the ground?
Or is that just me, with my mind spinning 'round?

As we water ideas, they sprout into laughs,
Like black holes at brunch sharing thoughts in their drafts.
Are dreams just stardust, tossed by cosmic chance?
In this dance of the silly, forget not to prance.

Wondering Along the Spiral Arms

In a galaxy full of quirks,
I ponder the stars and their works.
Why do ducks float in the sky?
Is it a dream, or just a lie?

Why do black holes wear a frown?
Do they suck in secrets, upside down?
I ask a comet passing by,
And it just winks, oh my, oh my!

Is space just a giant balloon?
Floating freely like a raccoon?
Why do planets dance in a line?
Do they rehearse? Is it divine?

I scribble thoughts, my mind a whirl,
Chasing stardust with a twirl.
What's the answer to the sun's bright beam?
Just a wink from the cosmos, it seems!

Whispers from the Edge of Time

Tick-tock goes the cosmic clock,
Wondering if squirrels can knock.
Do time travelers wear cool hats?
Or do they just dodge the chatting gnats?

I caught a whisper from the past,
A joke about a dinosaur's cast.
What if time's just a silly game?
Who keeps score? Is it the same?

Galaxies spin, and so do I,
Chasing shadows with a sigh.
Why do we dream in colors bright?
Could it be pizza that fuels our flight?

Oh dear clock, slow down your race,
Time's a trickster with a funny face.
What's next, a wormhole's silly ride?
Let's hope it takes us somewhere wide!

Cosmic Questions with No Answers

Why do shooting stars make a wish?
Is there a cosmic currency for this?
Do aliens celebrate their birthdays?
With cake made from cosmic splay?

Are meteors just really bad dreams?
Zooming fast with no moonbeams?
Why does my toaster burn bread so slow?
Maybe Einstein had a cat to bestow?

Do moons get lonely out in space?
Playing hide and seek in a dark place?
Why can't gravity take a break?
And let us hover like a pancake?

Questions swirl, like a galactic dust,
In the void, in wonders, we trust.
Why do socks disappear in the wash?
Is it a tumble of cosmic panache?

Philosophies of the Universe

What if atoms have a secret dance?
Twirling in the void, a cosmic chance.
Is the universe a giant joke?
With punchlines hidden in each smoke?

If stars could laugh, would they rain anew?
Wishing on dreams, they might just do.
Why's the sky painted deep navy blue?
Does it need a painter, just like you?

Do galaxies gossip, twinkling bright?
Trading tales through the vast flight.
Why do we think we're so advanced?
When ants do a jig as they prance?

Philosophy floats in the starlit air,
Prompting new questions from a cosmic chair.
Can we unravel this grand giggle?
Or is life just a cosmic wiggle?

Dark Matter of Life's Mysteries

In the cosmos deep and vast,
Questions swirl, a party cast.
Why do socks vanish from the wash?
Dark matter, or a sneaky nosh?

Some ponder fate, others, the cake,
Why do we laugh at every mistake?
Lost in thoughts like stars in flight,
Searching for answers, day and night.

The Light Years of Understanding

Light years stretch across the sky,
But why do donuts make us cry?
The mysteries of space might say,
It's the sprinkles that led us astray!

We ponder life's grand, silly prank,
Is it the universe, or just a tank?
Galaxies spin, much like our head,
What's for dinner? Let's not be fed!

Planets of Perspective

Planets float, each tale is spun,
Why do we all think it's just fun?
Mercury's fast, but why is it late?
Procrastination—it's a cosmic fate.

Humor in orbits, a laugh or two,
Why does Pluto feel so blue?
Adrift in space, or just a dream,
Finding the punchline in each cosmic beam.

Echoes from the Void

Listen close to the cosmic hum,
Why does life feel like bubblegum?
Floating thoughts in an empty space,
Searching for giggles in a serious race.

Echoes ring with a cheerful tone,
Why's a philosopher always alone?
Chasing questions like meteors fly,
A cosmic joke that makes us sigh.

The Silence Before Discovery

In the quiet of the night, a thought did creep,
"What if my socks are lost in the deep?"
My fridge hums secrets, my cat's in her zone,
While life's great mysteries sit on the phone.

Gravity winks as it pulls me right down,
While I ponder my lost left shoe, wearing a frown.
Stars giggle softly, their humor divine,
Who knew the questions could age like fine wine?

Behind every corner, the unknown waits there,
As I trip over answers, too silly to share.
The silence is rich, but it tickles my brain,
Like a burrito that's dancing, that's driving me sane.

Vortexes of Intrigue

In a swirl of confusion, my thoughts take a ride,
Like a rollercoaster, with joy as a guide.
Why do we laugh when it's really not neat?
Is the universe just one big cosmic tweet?

Questions like whirlwinds, they tug at my mind,
As I search for the truth that seems hard to find.
What's the meaning of life, oh where do I go?
Is it hidden in pizza? Might I need a dough?

Round and round in my head they do chase,
Each thought a teacup with a wild saucer face.
Why do dogs bark at their own special tail?
In the vortex of answers, it's comedy's trail.

The Radiance of Wonder

With a chuckle, I gaze at the starry night sky,
Wondering if aliens ever wave hi?
The twinkle of stars, like a cosmic joke,
While clumsy big planets just sway and provoke.

Behold the sun's shine, it glimmers and winks,
Does it laugh at the moon when it plays in the sinks?
What's life's greatest riddle? Might it be a jest?
Is the meaning of life just a big, goofy fest?

With each puff of clouds, my imagination plays,
As it morphs into shapes on whimsical days.
Could a rainbow be just a colorful lie?
The radiance of wonder, making questions fly!

Beyond the Event Horizon

What's lurking beyond where the light dares not glance?
Is it just odd socks? Or a great cosmic dance?
Beyond what we see, are we lost in a show?
Or is it just space taking its sweet time to flow?

Diving deep, I ponder each curious thought,
Have I misplaced my keys in the universe's lot?
Beneath the vast skies, my laughs start to bloom,
As I search high and low in this cosmic room.

Where questions explode, and giggles resound,
In the mystery of life, absurd truths abound.
So let's smile together and dance in this sphere,
For each question's a joy, let's give life a cheer!

Cosmic Echoes of the Past

In the void, did a donut go,
Caught in galaxies, spinning slow?
Did it ponder just what it meant,
To exist with a glaze and a sprinkle, bent?

Stars looked down with a wink and a grin,
Saying, 'Hey, you're not really a sin!'
Planets danced in an awkward waltz,
As meteors shouted, 'It's all your faults!'

From black holes to comets, they all had a say,
In this cosmic joke, let's laugh while we play.
Gravity teasingly pulls us all near,
And time laughs back, 'Why not have a beer?'

So next time you ponder the great unknown,
Remember those snacks that the universe owns.
With each cosmic giggle, let worries take flight,
Life's questions can sparkle, just hold on tight!

Refracted Realities

Lights in the sky bounce off the walls,
Twinkling like cats, just waiting for calls.
What do they know that we can't decide?
Maybe they're laughing, or taking a ride!

Through prisms of wonder, we squint and we strain,
Chasing those shadows like it's a game.
What shape is the truth, an octopus, a hat?
Or just a good story wrapped up in a cat?

Wormholes giggle, while we turn in thoughts,
Rattling our brains like cosmic robots.
Why is the sky blue? Or is it a trick?
Hope it's not just a bad cosmic flick!

Let's toast to the laughter that fills up the void,
To questions that swirl, and joys that we've enjoyed.
The real magic happens where wonders collide,
In refracted realities, where giggles abide!

The Celestial Mind

Floating in space with a curious thought,
Did gravity ever get tied in a knot?
Saturn's rings are just hula hoops,
For playful moons and their cosmic troops!

Stars throw a party, no need for a theme,
And time is the punch, a wobbly dream.
Einstein might chuckle at all of our quirks,
While black holes provide the best of the perks!

Nebula balloons drift with silly designs,
As comets post memes on their starlit signs.
With every new question that floats through the air,
Let's giggle and dance like we just don't care!

So, lift up your glasses to the skies above,
The universe winks, as if sending love.
In the realm where sanity often unwinds,
Let's sail through the cosmos, with the celestial mind!

Horizons of Hope

Out past the stars, what wonders await?
Is it life or just breakfast on a giant plate?
Each twinkling light could be a friendly face,
Or a cosmic burrito floating in space!

Fuzzy green aliens taking a stroll,
With ice cream cones made from a meteor's roll.
They ponder our planets and drink cosmic tea,
Debating if peanut butter's the best gift to be!

If time has a schedule, it's lost at the party,
Where nobody's worried and all things are hearty.
Hope swirls in laughter like cosmic confetti,
As we chase the horizons, our dreams always ready!

So dream of the stars, and sail through the night,
With funny ideas that are vibrant and bright.
In this grand adventure where questions arise,
We'll feast on the wonders that fill up our skies!

Echoes in the Cosmic Dance

In the void, I ask, where's my sock?
Did it float off on a space rock?
Planets spin, and I'm just here,
Wondering why I have no beer.

Are comets just cosmic candy bars?
I tried to reach one, but it's too far.
Stars blink and giggle, what a sight,
As I trip over my own satellite.

Why is gravity such a clingy friend?
Pulling my snacks? This should end!
I ponder these things with my cat,
Who thinks the universe is just a mat.

As I chase dreams like shooting stars,
I find myself lost at interstellar bars.
With laughter echoing through the night,
I toast to questions, and the cosmic plight.

From Dust to Dreams

Once a speck in the stellar dust,
Now I search for my next snack's crust.
Life's a journey, or so they say,
But where's the GPS on this wild display?

Galaxies swirling like my morning brew,
I spill it often, don't know what to do.
Creating chaos, just to be bold,
Yet here I cough, on the secrets untold.

Stardust settles on my sandwich bread,
Do they toast it up? Or is it just said?
Questions rise like the sun in the east,
Should I write a book? Or just have a feast?

From atoms to snacks, I make my stand,
The universe giggles, isn't it grand?
As dreams float by like balloons in the air,
I chase them down with a hopeful glare.

The Universe's Unanswered Call

Ringing in space, is that a phone?
Hello, it's me, you're not alone!
But who picks up in the vacuum wide?
It's a cosmic prank, let's take it in stride.

Planets wobble with a comical flair,
As I ask, "Do aliens drink ginger ale?"
Life's puzzling hiccups mix with the beams,
Echoing laughter in infinite themes.

Black holes lurking, with their sly grin,
Do they suck up the knowledge I'm in?
Or are they just saving space for a snack,
Munching on secrets as they hit the track?

Stars twinkle back, in their playful way,
And I can't help but ask, "Can I stay?"
In this circus of questions, absurd and bright,
I find my joy in the cosmic delight.

Celestial Questions

What if the moon has a secret jam?
A rock star hideaway, oh, how glam!
I'd dance with stars if I could, it's true,
While planets hum a tune just for you.

In the Milky Way, my thoughts take flight,
Like a comet escaping into the night.
But where's the end of this cosmic race?
I'd like to know, with a smile on my face.

Is the sun just a glorified light bulb?
Warming up planets with an embarrassing lube?
Or is it selling sun tan lotion in space,
To keep all the aliens in perfect grace?

Questions bubble up like soda from the can,
Each fizz a riddle, a spark of a plan.
As I ponder the universe's delight,
I can't help but chuckle at the stars tonight.

Unraveled Dimensions

In a universe so vast, oh dear,
I wonder where my socks disappear!
Galaxies spin, while I just sit,
Pondering why my coffee's never lit.

Einstein claimed time's just a trick,
But my watch seems to disagree, quick!
A black hole might swallow my last slice,
Of pizza—oh, that would not be nice!

Atoms dance in a quantum ballet,
While I trip over my shoes every day.
Do stars gossip about my blunders?
Or is that just gravity's thunder?

In dimensions unseen, I lose my keys,
Blame it on space, if you please.
Life's questions tumble, float, and spin,
Is it too late to call it a win?

Philosophical Orbits

In circles we move, why not in squares?
Questions orbiting like cosmic flares.
Is there life out in the deep blue?
Or do aliens watch reality shows too?

Gravity pulls, but with wings I'd soar,
Yet here I am, stuck at the grocery store.
Is broccoli really from outer space?
Or just a green blob with a funny face?

Wormholes lead where the snacks are free,
I'd travel dimensions for a cup of tea.
Einstein's equations, I might just ignore,
If it means I can find a pizza door.

Laugh at the cosmos, it laughs back once,
Between here and there, it never puns.
Every thought's a twinkling starry jest,
In the orbit of questions, we just do our best!

Celestial Musings

Stars blink knowingly, who do they see?
My deep thoughts on toast, wasting coffee with glee.
Are clouds just cotton candy in the sky?
And do raindrops drop out to try the dry?

The moon's a big cheese, they say with a grin,
Do astronauts munch on it; would they begin?
In every black hole lie lost socks and dreams,
And echoes of laughter that burst at the seams.

Planets are spinning, their tunes off-key,
While I dance silly, just me, oh me!
If Venus had people, would they sing quips?
Or would it be frowns and mismatched trips?

Galactic giggles burst through the night,
As cosmic clowns offer popcorn delight.
Let's ride on a comet, or at least take a chance,
At the grand cosmic show, let's all laugh and dance!

Pondering the Void

The void is wide, yet I feel so small,
Can I fit my doubts in a cosmic ball?
When I trip on a thought, it flies through the air,
Does it laugh at my tumble and playful despair?

Questions are like meteors, zooming so fast,
Will they land softly, or shatter at last?
Is the universe a joke, told by the wise?
Or just a prankster in an absurd disguise?

Time is a river that flows without care,
While I sit by the bank, with existential flair.
Do galaxies giggle at choices I make?
Or are they too busy in their own high stakes?

In the echo of silence, I chuckle and grin,
For each riddle I face, I'll bravely dive in.
With cosmic laughter, the questions go round,
In the vastness of nothing, joy can be found!

Echoes of Existence

Why does toast always fall down?
Is it fate or just the ground?
Do socks have a secret life?
Plotting escapes, causing strife?

When cats stare at the wall,
Are they hearing nature's call?
Do plants enjoy a good chat?
Minds blown, just imagine that!

If goldfish could dance, oh my!
Would they twirl and leap so high?
What wisdom do old trees keep?
Do they dream in roots and sleep?

This cosmic joke we live in,
Leaves us laughing through our grin.
With each giggle, we explore,
Life's questions, who could want more?

Fragments of Forever

What if chairs have feelings too?
Crushed by humans, oh what to do?
Do we owe them an apology?
Or just let them sit and be?

Why does every sock go missing?
Are they in a world just kissing?
With unmatched friends in the dark,
Planning a trip to the park?

If a dog talks behind our back,
What mischief would he unpack?
Sharing gossip with the cat?
Oh glory, imagine that spat!

As we ponder these silly schemes,
Life's a wild ride, with wacky dreams.
So giggle at the cosmic dance,
In this universe of happenstance.

Celestial Conundrums

Stars blink twice, what do they mean?
Are they winking at me unseen?
Do they gossip about our nights?
Trading tales of cosmic flights?

Why do we count sheep to sleep?
Have they secrets they won't keep?
Do they come from the moon's light?
Frolicking softly in the night?

If life had a manual we could read,
Would it be full of silly creed?
With sections on why cats are sly,
And why donuts make us fly?

In these puzzles, let's take a look,
Grab your quill, write your own book.
Bursting bubbles of laughter and fun,
Finding joy in questions, everyone!

Infinity's Riddle

What if mirrors are time machines?
Reflecting worlds of magical scenes?
Were you ever a famous queen?
Or a fish with a sparkly sheen?

If each hiccup is time's embrace,
Do we dance in a fragile space?
What do giggles taste like, pray?
A sprinkle of joy in the fray?

Can we ask clouds why they drift?
Or why they give the sky a lift?
Do rainbows get lost and confused?
In a swirl of colors, amused?

So raise a glass to the absurd,
In each question, feel the word.
Life's riddle is what makes us shine,
Laughing together through this design!

From Stars to Sentience

In the vastness, a big boom,
Did a star just drop its broom?
Life begins, but what's the cost?
Did the universe just get lost?

Are we here for laughs or sighs?
Did the planets roll their eyes?
Creation's joke, or cosmic play?
What's for dinner—black holes or sway?

With each quasar, a mystery,
Did Einstein nap through history?
We ponder moons and celestial pies,
While space dust winks, oh how it pries!

So let's toast to this grand mess,
With questions we can't confess.
For in the chaos, laughter reigns,
And joy amidst the cosmic grains.

The Infinite Inquiry

Why does the sun wear shades of gold?
Did planets whine when they grew old?
Cosmic riddles in endless flight,
"Hey, who's that?"—another satellite!

Do black holes have a cozy nook?
Is there life in every nook?
Galaxies swirl, but can they dance?
Or are they stuck in a cosmic trance?

Did comets tell tales of their trips?
And aliens eat with cyber chips?
In a universe so wide and vast,
Did time's clock just break and outlast?

So as we ponder the whys and hows,
Let's giggle and scratch our brows.
For in the cosmos, full of quirks,
Laughter's the key amid the jerks.

Notes from the Cosmos

Dear Earthling, are you there?
Tell me, do you have a care?
From stars that twinkle, oh so bright,
To black holes that gulp the night.

Did a supernova just sneeze?
Or is it stardust with the peas?
What's with aliens and their hats?
Do they plan intergalactic chats?

Space dust bunnies, floating free,
Are they hiding—let's take a spree!
And what of galaxies lost in time?
Have they forgotten their own rhyme?

So here's a note from me to you,
Let's giggle at the grand review.
For in this cosmos, wild and wide,
Life's questions are the ultimate ride.

Interstellar Introspection

Did gravity go to the gym?
Or is it just forever dim?
The stars are laughing; do you hear?
What's the meaning—another beer?

Are asteroids just angry rocks?
And comets, do they wear adult socks?
In this cosmic theater of the absurd,
Did the universe just flip a bird?

Why does time never seem to stop?
Is it playing an interstellar prop?
We ponder deeply while fish fly high,
What's the deal with that big guy?

So raise your glass, let's toast the stars,
To questions that drive us to Mars.
For in this life, one thing is true,
Laughter is the glue that binds me and you.

The Universe Within Us

In the darkness, a spark ignites,
Questions dance like fireflies at night.
What's for dinner in the cosmic scheme?
Is Pluto just playing hard to beam?

Galaxies spin, each twist a joke,
When stars collide, do they just poke?
Wormholes made for silly fun,
Or just portals to where we've run?

Life's a riddle, a twisty affair,
Are aliens living in your hair?
So many queries, each one bizarre,
Do socks vanish with a mini star?

Asteroids chuckle as they whiz by,
Stars wink at us from the sky.
What's the answer to all this play?
Just query the cosmos at the end of the day!

Cosmic Whispers

Twirling planets in a grand ballet,
Whisper secrets, but in a playful way.
Do black holes suck in the good or bad?
Or is it all just interstellar glad?

Comets giggle as they race each other,
Shooting stars ask, 'What's the big bother?'
Life's a quiz with no cheat sheet near,
Do aliens laugh, or do they just sneer?

Stardust delicately sprinkles our path,
Do moons tell tales with giggles and laughs?
Questions float like balloons in the sky,
Are we the punchline? Oh my, oh my!

The cosmos grins, it's quite the joke,
Do meteors cry, or just stoke?
As we ponder the vastness above,
Let's enjoy each riddle, and share the love!

Nebula of Uncertainty

In a cloud of thought, where humor blooms,
Questions dart like playful loons.
Is the universe large, or just in our heads?
And what do stars do when they go to bed?

Nebulas swirl, but are they shy?
Do they giggle when comets fly by?
Is life just a cosmic game of tag?
Or perhaps a simulation by a quirkier rag?

Floating thoughts, like dust on a breeze,
Are we merely shadows among the trees?
Astrophysics with a side of cheer,
What's the answer? Maybe life's just beer!

The universe chuckles, it likes to tease,
Questions come easily, like popping peas.
In this cosmic mess, let laughter reign,
For a life that's funny is never mundane!

Starborn Queries

From stardust springs the questions we seek,
Are we the daring, or just the weak?
Do moons envy the sun's shining show?
Or is it all one cosmic flow?

Galaxies giggle in clusters and beams,
What's for lunch? The cosmos dreams.
Do time travelers chuckle inside a loop?
Or are they just stuck in an endless scoop?

Meteor showers rain down thought,
Are dreams what the aliens never bought?
Queries like fireworks light up the night,
Is life a joke or a serious fright?

So ponder away, in this starry delight,
With laughter as fuel, we'll take flight.
In the depths of the cosmos, we search for the clue,
And maybe it's just having fun with you!

Cosmic Whispers of Existence

In the dark, what's that sound?
A cat thinking it's profound.
Stars giggle, light-years away,
As they play hide and seek each day.

Why does gravity give me a frown?
Is it why my pants slide down?
The cosmos laughs, with twinkling eyes,
While I ponder cake and pies.

Are aliens really just shy?
Hiding out, oh me, oh my!
Perhaps they're on a searching spree,
For snacks and some quality tea.

By night, I can't help but wonder,
Is the moon just a giant blunder?
It's cheese, they say, that's the trick,
Yet I still can't find a quick fix.

A Universe of Inquiries

Why do socks disappear in pairs?
Is it space's way of declaring shares?
Every wash feels like a battle,
With missing mates in cosmic rattle.

Do stars get tired of their glow?
Do they take naps, just to show?
What if planets take a day off?
'They should!' I say, with a scoff.

Can comets really dance in the void?
Is that why they seem so overjoyed?
Each flicker a giggle, a playful tease,
Nature's way of laughing with ease.

What if time met a bag of chips?
Would it crunch with every word it flips?
Ideas swirl like nebula bliss,
In the universe's comic twist.

Starlit Echoes of Curiosity

When did time start ticking loud?
Did a clock join a dancing crowd?
Or was it just a sleepy cat,
Deciding to have a chat?

Are black holes secretly shy?
Sucking in things like a fry?
Maybe they just want to share,
All the stuff they've sucked in there.

Do meteors cry when they fall?
Is space a big, comfy stall?
Where wishes are carved in dust,
And dreams are grounded, in stardust rust.

Is the universe just one big joke?
With giggles in every smoke?
What if each planet was a clown?
Wobbling joyfully, upside down?

Infinite Threads of Wonder

Why does the sky wear a blue hat?
Is it to hide from a curious rat?
Clouds fluffing like pillows in flight,
Might they be softies, just out of sight?

What are stars wishing upon at night?
Maybe for pizza, just to ignite?
Or a party with planets, a cosmic spree,
Where waves of joy float merrily.

Can a quasar laugh like I do?
Or is it just a light show, too?
If they giggled with each brightness gleam,
Would they all come together and dream?

What's in a black hole's deep embrace?
A cosmic vacuum, or a hidden place?
I'll bet it's where all lost socks go,
Joining a dance to a secret show.

www.ingramcontent.com/pod-product-compliance
Lightning Source LLC
Chambersburg PA
CBHW071851160426
43209CB00003B/514